WALKING TH
OF THE MII

VOLUME T1

By

Michael R. Kettle

The Northern half of the Staffordshire and Worcestershire Canal and part of the Shropshire Union Canal from its junction with the S and W at Autherley to Tyrley Locks near Market Drayton.

ENGLISH OAK   SW

Walking the Canals of the Midlands
Volume Three

copyright © Michael R Kettle 2001
ISBN 1 903607 07 8

Front cover picture: The Author during one of our walks.
Rear cover watercolour: Avenue Bridge, Shropshire Union Canal.

Watercolours, Nature drawings, and some photographs by
S.Walters, remainder of photographs by the author.

Published in Great Britain by
Able Publishing
13 Station Road
Knebworth
Hertfordshire
SG3 6AP

Tel: (01438) 812320 / 814316
Fax: (01438) 815232

Email: fp@ablepublishing.co.uk
Website: www.ablepublishing.co.uk

Acknowledgments and Dedications

Map Extracts from GEOprojects' maps of the Staffordshire and Worcestershire Canal and the Shropshire Union Canal with the permission of the publisher GEOprojects (UK) Ltd. Tel: 0118 939 3567, Fax: 0118 959 8283, email: enquiries@geoprojects.demon.co.uk. © Crown copyright.

I am also most grateful to Ordnance Survey office for their permission to refer to their Landranger products.

This book is dedicated to the Inland Waterways Association, and to British Waterways, without whose untiring efforts little or no canal walks would be possible. Also to the various Canal Societies for their preservation of our heritage.

My sincere thanks to purchasers of my first two volumes, and for their encouraging remarks.

Most of all I dedicate this work to Sheila, in thanks for her company on all the walks, in all weathers, and for her paintings which have given life to my words.

Whilst every effort to ensure the accuracy of detail has been made, changes may have taken place since our original walks. We feel certain that any such variation will not spoil your exercise and enjoyment.

CONTENTS

INTRODUCTION

Having had a very satisfactory response to the first two books in this series of walking Midland canals, and wishing to cover other important waterways in the region, we now offer further walks for those who would like to enjoy the peace of rural Staffordshire and Shropshire.

We already covered the Southern part of the Staffordshire and Worcestershire Canal, designed by James Brindley, in volume 1. Now, we offer the Northern section, from where it links with the Shropshire Union, at Autherley Junction, to Great Haywood, where it connects with another Brindley Canal, the Trent and Mersey.

A complete route is thus available to narrow boats from the River Severn to Liverpool, and the River Mersey. However, walkers will be satisfied to cover the various walks up to the junction at Great Haywood.

The second section of this book, offers the charm of Thomas Telford's masterpiece, the Shropshire Union, popularly known as the 'Shroppie', but originally designated the Birmingham and Liverpool Canal. This was created by the merging of several waterways, and eventually reaches Wales, or Liverpool via the City of Chester.

The two canals are very different, each created in a style by which their designers were best known. The Brindley meander along the edge of River valleys, using locks to overcome height variations. The Telford 'cut and thrust' in a direct line, creating cuttings and embankments, and avoiding locks, except when all else failed.

We hope you enjoy these walks as much as we did, and suggest that you do not just consider walking as a summer activity. Try a crisp, colourful autumn stroll with leaves crunching beneath your feet, a frosty winter's day, when the edges of the path are white, or a bright day in spring, when the trees are in bud, and birdsong at its height. Every season has something to offer, and you will remember your canal walks with pleasure.

Always dress according to the weather. Towpaths can be cold and windy, especially in open country areas. Footwear too, is most important. Waterproof boots, or even wellingtons, are recommended, but most of all, make sure they are comfortable.

Happy walking.

Michael R. Kettle

JAMES BRINDLEY

1716 - 1772

Surveyor and Engineer for the Staffs/Worcs Canal

Part One

The Northern section of the Staffordshire and Worcestershire Canal, from Autherley Junction to Great Haywood, a total distance of 21 Miles.

Anyone who has read and walked with Book 1, covering the lower part of this canal, from Stourport to Autherley, will be familiar with the Brindley style of canal design. That entails the use of natural land features, such as River Valleys, to avoid large numbers of tunnels and locks. In fact, through 48 Miles of canal, there are only 40 locks. This also reduced the total cost of the entire length to £100,000.

In many areas, you will see that the waterway runs along the edge of natural rocky outcrops, and that the opposite side of the canal falls away to lower ground.

At Compton, on the outskirts of Wolverhampton, where the first turf was cut to commence the canal, the ground is level, and forms a plateau. This is the highest point and locks leading to it, from either side, climb upwards.

The Staffs/Worcs was opened in 1772, but unfortunately James Brindley died before the event, at the comparatively young age of 55. However, since he was involved in a large number of other canal projects, it is likely that Samuel Simcock (Brindley's brother in law), and Thomas Dadford were very much involved in the engineering. A total of 42 bridges cross this waterway and the canal itself crosses several aqueducts, although only two, both in the Great Haywood area, are of any real interest. The final one, at Great Haywood which carries the canal over the River Trent, is the most notable, and is definitely of Brindley design.

The Act of Parliament required for the construction of the Staffs/Worcs, was, by coincidence, passed on the same day (14th May 1766) as Brindley's other major work, The Trent and Mersey.

Section 1

Autherley Junction to Slade Heath
3½ Miles

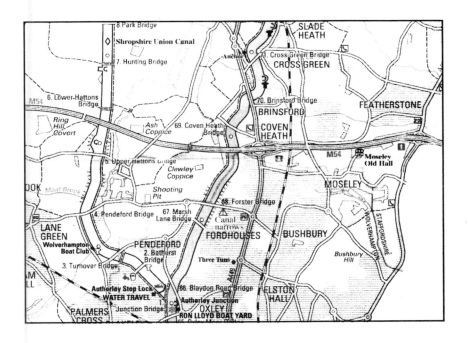

Autherley Junction is about three miles North West of Wolverhampton, and is best reached from the A449 Trunk Rd signposted Stafford from Wolverhampton Ring Road. This road has already passed through Worcester and Kidderminster, so anyone travelling from those areas, simply follows the A449. From Bridgnorth, the A454 reaches the starting point, via Compton, Tettenhall, and Pendeford, whilst the M54 from Telford joins the A449 at Junction 2, the route then follows the A449 Southward. Except for those on A454, turn off the main road at Fordhouses, following the sign for Pendeford, until reaching Oxley.

Ordnance Survey Landranger Map no 139, Map Ref 903020 is your destination. There is some parking in side roads nearby, whilst West Midland Buses, or the railway station at Bilbrook (Codsall), are possible to enable you to reach the start.

On arrival at Autherley, you will find access to two canals, and you need to follow signs for the Staffs/Worcs. A wide expanse of water at the junction, and a good towpath crosses the S.U. by means of a high bridge, however if you park on the verge of the main road, there is easy access to the towpath. Turn northwards, and the path is mainly grass covered. There is, however a surfaced path running parallel with the towpath, from which any activity on the water can be seen.

Our first walk took place in late summer on a day when the breeze was strong enough to show the backs of the leaves, and ripple the surface of the water. The width of channel here, is average, and the edges are modern metal plates. We have left the conurbation behind except for housing estates and one or two schools. An allotment fringes the far bank, and behind that, a thin line of sturdy poplars shield a large sportsground from the eyes of passers-by. A slight left turn, and we are heading for the first bridge of this walk, an older style, carrying pedestrian traffic only.

We have seen our first ducks, in small groups.

Faced with the choice of walking either along the towpath or the better surface of the path a few yards distant, also heading towards the bridge, we chose the grass covered original canal-side path. In places, this has crumbled into the water, leaving some holes, but we do not find any problem in following an original route.

I have just commented into my dictating machine that there only seem to be small groups of duck, when seven appear. These look as if they are the young of this year, because, though large, they look as if their feathers are still downy. On the far side, one or two properties have gardens to the waters edge, and some boats, privately owned are moored there.

Marsh Lane Bridge, no 67 is now close, and the secondary path has risen to pass over it. Anyone who has opted for that route, must now return to the towpath, to pass beneath the bridge. Here, we see a pair of Swans, with four cygnets crossing the canal to search for food. Once again, it is apparent that from their dark colour, and downy appearance, they must be this years brood. However, they are already the same size as their parents. We love to see these families, and feel it is a good omen for the day.

After the low bridge, at which point, the path is earth covered, we are soon into one of the narrowest sections of any canal we have walked so far. Rocks line the far side, and the edge of the path, so the Engineers must have used dynamite at this point.

This section, no wider than a lock, is two hundred yards in length, with one short passing place, half way along. The narrow length finishes at Forster Bridge, no 68, but the bridge is more like a tunnel, being extra wide, and the width of path is rather confined. A little eerie, and it reminds us of the tunnel at Cookley, except that that one has a handrail along its edge.

The narrow canal has not widened, until after this bridge, but we can see the wider water. Once beyond the bridge, it is a little like walking through a cutting, and on a windy day, there is definitely shelter.

We can hear the sound of industry above, and to our right, but it is not intrusive. Since we are well past Wolverhampton, we are surprised to find any form of commerce, at all, but there are a number of trees on both sides, those on our side, are hanging over the path, whilst on the opposite bank, they help to screen any buildings. A trio of Mallard rest on a severed tree trunk, which lies in the channel at this point. It does not seem to be a real hazard, and is large enough to be seen by boaters.

There is now a little industry on our side too, with the rusty remnants of a metal fence, along the edge. The likelihood of a Wharf at this point, is considered, and we decide this was possible.

We have seen several craft, making their way back towards Autherley Junction, the usual cheery greetings have been exchanged. The canal turns slightly to the right, then, in a longer curve, to the left. The only sound now, is the wind in the trees. Ground to the left is marshy, and some small streams carry overflow water from the canal. Loose leaves have collected on the surface into one small area, by the wind, and the surface of the canal is rippled where not shielded from the strong breeze.

A new bridge, unnumbered due to its recent installation, and carrying the ever hustling traffic of the M54, crosses the waterway, reminding us of a world beyond the peace and tranquillity, we now enjoy. Beyond the fields on the far side, the A449 trunk road still conveys heavy traffic, even though the various motorways were designed to reduce much of it. This main artery carries traffic from Stafford to Wolverhampton, or vice-versa.

We now find open fields to our left, with a clear view to the West, for some distance. The first Angler seen so far today, sits on the bank, in anticipation, his Bicycle close at hand, for he is well away from any community.

As the canal curves to the right, we pass beneath Coven Heath Bridge, no 69, an old bridge, somewhat in need of repair. Even so, it carries local and farm traffic. A Kestrel hovers close to the path, turns, then hovers once more, I hope he finds a tasty lunch.

Away to the right, there is a small group of mobile homes, in a secluded park, and a few ordinary houses, a little distance further on. The towpath is variable. Some sections are modern and firm, whilst others are grass covered. There is also variation in width, but we have no problems with walking.

Along this part of the canal, we notice that the water is very dark, almost like peat laden Scottish waters, but surrounding land does not suggest this to be the case in Staffordshire.

A turn of 90 degrees takes us under bridge no 70, at Brinsford. From there, boats are moored along the far bank, privately owned, in the main. Some have sheds and small gardens along reserved spaces. The standard of boats here, is very high, some unusual in

14

design. This is the Coven Cruising Club.

We follow the waterway into a slow left hand curve. Other boats are passing through the area, and the towpath is good to walk. After passing the final boat moored in the section, we see to our left a Golf course. To our right, beyond a large winding hole, are open fields. We are now approaching bridge no 71, Cross Green Bridge, and note that all round us country activities, and animals are predominant. Thoroughbred horses and free range chickens are included.

Many properties on the far side, have gardens down to the edge of the canal, and we note with some surprise that the bridge was built in 1822, almost 50 years after the canal was opened. It is in some need of work on it's brickwork, especially as a quite busy road crosses here.

The waterway winds to the right, and passes close to the "Anchor" Inn, which is now a Steak Bar. It is a popular stopping place for boats, and we are almost sorry it is too early for lunch.

British Waterways operatives were renewing the towpath, as we passed, and we received the customary pleasant greeting. In fact, I would be really surprised if we were to meet miserable BW employees. Several craft are already moored along the stretch, both private and hired, whilst more private boats are tied up on the start of a very large turn, a little distance along, on the far side.

Coven, a small community, is to our left, and we are soon close to our last bridge of the walk, Slade Heath Bridge no 72. Over it runs a very busy road, and the path is narrow, under the low headroom. As the canal once more turns left, we sit on a wall, have our lunch, then return to Autherley.

Early Morning on the Staffs / Worcs Canal

Old Tollhouse, Gailey Wharf

Section 2

Slade Heath to Gailey Wharf
4 Miles

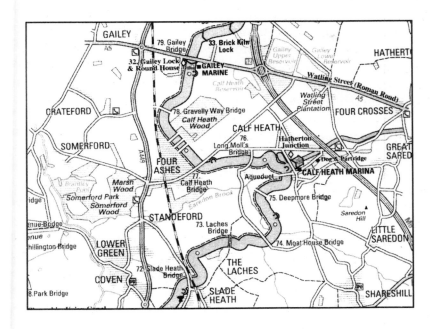

To commence a walk from Slade Heath, you will find that your own transport would be best. Buses are available, but enquiries should be made at Wolverhampton Tourist Office, or West Midland Travel.

Directions to the starting point, for using own transport, is as follows. From Wolverhampton, Kidderminster, Stourbridge take A449 Northbound (signpost Stafford). From Stafford, the A449 Southbound is required. Motorway users should leave M6 and join the M54, then leave that Motorway at Junction 2. About 3/4 of a mile North of M54 Junction 2, take a turn to Cross Green. Pass over the canal, and in just under 1/2 mile, you will reach Slade Heath. There is limited parking on the side of the road.

Ordnance Survey Map sheet 139 is required, Map Ref is 919066. Almost adjoining the canal bridge you require, is the main line Railway, to help identify the correct start.

Pass below the two bridges, once you are on the towpath, which is grass covered. Over the water are two modernised cottages, one having two Milk Churns, and two old washing Mangles. One of these properties is called "The Wharf".

Already, we have turned to the left, and along the path there is a thick hedge of Conifers. Another small group of houses are in a small cul de sac, their gardens on the water's edge. The area is peaceful, although, on turning further to the left, the route heads back towards the railway, along which you will see numerous trains, both passenger and freight. One or two farms lie over the fields on the far side, and the towpath is narrow, and has been allowed to grow wild.

For a short distance, the canal straightens. The far bank is lined with modem metal links, thus indicating that BW have been bringing the area up to standard. Martins are swooping over the water, gathering insects from close to the surface, whilst Starlings gather in groups on nearby wires. There are also many Pigeons in evidence, so we are able to watch the various types of bird at their activities.

Looking across the fields, at the left of our walk, we can see some form of industrial complex. There is a flame burning at the top of a high chimney, which reminds us of an oil refinery. The canal is quite wide, and shortly meanders to the right. On the far side, trees are forming a screen, but all of them are a few feet from the bank. Behind them, Horses canter in the fields, and further on, farm buildings can be seen.

The hedge which divided path from field, on our side, has now ended, and that field is full of straw bales. An empty barn, just a few yards away, may soon be filled. Already we feel the coming of autumn. Trees are beginning to turn colour, the atmosphere is mellow, and high clouds threaten some rain, though not at once. A dark wood lines the far bank, full of a variety of deciduous trees, including several Sweet Chestnuts, their laden branches overhanging the water. A small group of young canoeists gather in a small clearing, their coloured safety hats brightening the gloom of the wood. However, we have passed before they take to the water.

Beyond the wood, we turn right again, a large field now covering the area. We pass below Laches Bridge, no 73, and the canal turns several times, in an erratic, even uncertain course. The fields have numerous sheep, and concrete edging now lines the far bank.

Just around another right hand bend, we discover a pair of freight carrying boats, bearing British Waterways colours. Both boats were built in Rickmansworth, the home of so many of the earlier cargo carrying craft. Unfortunately, there is no crew to talk to, to discover their history, so we plod on. This part of the canal is quite secluded, with trees on both sides. We reach Moat House Bridge no 74, and although there is a large house just across the field, we cannot say whether or not, that is the Moat House.

As we turn again, this time to the left, we find a moored boat being renovated by a young man. Nothing strange in that, you may think, but the boat is in the middle of nowhere, and any materials he may require, must be brought some distance. We cross an overflow, and note that by it, is a sandstone marker. It is about 30" high, has at least one letter inscribed near the top, but there is no clue on the map as to the significance of the object.

Elderberries hang in large tempting bunches, from nearby trees. This further sign of the approach of autumn ought to bear a notice 'pick me', rather like Alice in Wonderland.

Bridge no 75, either Deepmoor, or Deepmore, according to

the map one uses, is close by. One or two Pigeons fly around it, and in one of my 'psychic' moments, I say that this looks like good Heron country. As if on cue, we see one of these graceful birds taking off from the bank, flying on a parallel course, though in the opposite direction to us. We have not seen one for several walks, so this is most pleasing. Almost immediately, a boat passes beneath the bridge, and we ask if the crew saw 'him'. They shout back that they have followed that bird for some time.

We turned left at the bridge, but now enter a very steep right-hander. This is a pretty section of the canal, which looks somewhat familiar, although we had never walked here previously. The 'deja vu' is caused by the similarity of a stretch of canal between Stourton, and Brierley Hill. on the Stourbridge Canal, and the one we now walk. This occurs from time to time and is due to similar terrain through which different waterways pass.

Now the path is wider, and obviously more used. Trees are overhanging the towpath, but the canal still meanders, firstly one way, then the other. Right in the centre of the channel, a family of swans, two parents, four cygnets, are resting. We wonder if they are the same ones, we saw on a previous walk, on this same canal, but cannot be certain.

As we turn left, yet again, we see a group of boats, moored on the far side. A notice tells us that the gardens belong to "Misty's", a very pleasant eating house, which we later found offered a very good menu both at lunchtime, and in the evening. Boats are able to moor nearby, and there is access from the road, but walkers need to pass over a small aqueduct, then across a footbridge, and through a metal gate.

This Bar and Restaurant is situated on the corner of the old 'Hatherton' branch, once a link between the Staffs/Worcs, and the BCN, but now closed at the second lock. However, with such a wide entrance, one might be fooled into believing that it was still open.

Beyond the branch, the Hatherton Marina is full of boats, and the road close by leads to Calf Heath. The Marina is for boats which are privately owned, and is neat and tidy. Other craft may moor at the canal edge.

We follow the grass covered towpath, first left, then right past the moorings and the Marina, heading for the edge of a small wood. On reaching this, the canal hairpins and the wood is left behind. Now we are walking through open fields, large paddocks with horses, to the right, fallow ground on our left. Both sides of the canal have been reinforced with metal plates, but for some little while, there have been no water birds of any kind, not even a solitary duck.

The canal swings in different directions, typically Brindley I feel. We have reached Long Moll's Bridge, no 76, carrying only a farm lane. We wonder who, and what Long Moll, may have been, the most obvious suggestion, an unusually tall local lady, but no-one to ask. Beyond the bridge, an unusual straight line of water, with overhanging trees over the path. Many of them are willows, now shedding leaves, and other types of trees have dropped their dead leaves onto the water.

The canal had narrowed for the bridge, and now widens out once more. Breezes ruffle the water, and a gap in the trees, produces a whitish reflection on the calmer waters, contrasting with dark brown, in other parts of the water.

We are still passing farmland to our right, and heathland to our left, and a scattering of buildings tell us that we are approaching Calf Heath. However, we discover a different landscape, on our arrival beyond Calf Heath Bridge no 77, for the Chemical works we had seen earlier, is now close to the canal, on the left.

Anglers are in evidence, ignoring the industrial presence, their umbrellas spread like so many green mushrooms, awaiting the possibility of rain. I am bound to say that the close proximity of the works, fails to spoil the walk. A fairly substantial hedge is a shield.

We have never been far from the main railway line, since the start of the walk, but now it has closed in, due to the various twists and turns of the waterway. Passing under three modern bridge structures, the towpath widens, and has lost it's grass surface, due to more constant use. Only a few yards after the railway comes close, the canal turns away from it, as if they had quarrelled, and passes under Gravelly Way Bridge, no 78, the last numbered bridge this side of Gailey.

Calf Heath Wood, stands a short distance over to the right, and by comparison with recent woods, looks quite large. Three more turns, two left, and one right, brings us to the final yards to Gailey Wharf. This is straight, and moored boats can be seen there. A mere handful of houses are seen here, and a boatyard is at Gailey itself.

A rest, possibly some refreshment, and a look around the excellent shop at Gailey (a former toll house), will set you up for your return walk. Public transport is restricted to buses, the nearest station still three miles away, a possible alternative is to be met here by someone with a car, for there is parking to the rear of the shop, and it is easy to locate, sited close to the A5 road. We walked back, and enjoyed seeing all interesting things, from the opposite direction.

Hatherton Junction showing disused arm

British Waterways Boats on Staffs/Worcs at Slade Green

Deepmoor (Deepmore) Bridge

BEECH

S.W.

24

Section 3

Gailey to Longford Lock, Penkridge
3 Miles

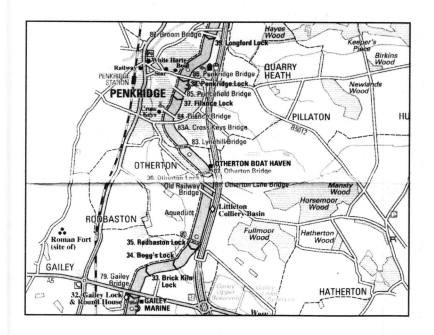

Gailey Wharf is probably one of the most straightforward starting points to find. To locate it, you require Ordnance Survey Landranger Map, sheet 127, map ref 920105. If travelling on the M6 Motorway, you need Junction 12, then take A5 Westbound, past Calf Heath Reservoir, approx ½ mile to the wharf. Using M54, leave at Junction 2, A449 Northbound (Stafford) right onto A5, at Gailey roundabout, for a mere few yards. A449 travellers also turn onto A5, Eastwards at Gailey roundabout.

Look for the distinctive shape of the round Toll House, on the left if coming from M6, on right from other routes. The car park is reached by a short drive, to the right of the house, and is adjacent to it.

We arrived at Gailey, on a sunny morning in early October. There was a magic in the air, that indefinable something which makes the difference between an indifferent day, and a good one. The sun was reflecting back from the weathered mellow bricks of the round tower, several boats were leaving overnight moorings. Everyone seemed full of happiness.

We visited the well-stocked, and extremely tidy shop, below the tower, and were spoiled by the range of goods available, Well worth a visit, at either end of the walk.

Gailey lock, is the first since Compton, some way back down the canal, and also the first dropping down through pretty Staffordshire countryside heading for Great Haywood. Brindley reduced the need for locks, by using natural contours, but added to the distances.

With so many beautifully kept boats on the canals, it is perhaps unfair to pick any one out for special mention, However, I make an exception, for, not only decorated canal-ware, but the brightness of the paint, and not least for the name itself "Jenny Wren". The owners were very pleased to be praised for their efforts, and as with most owners, a friendly chat ensued.

After the lock, the waterway swings left, then right before passing through open fields. High up, on new electricity cables, the man with a fantastic view, waved down to us lesser mortals. Having no head for heights, I did not envy him his perch right up one of the new pylons, and just returned his wave.

Here, the canal is wide, and soon we see the next lock Brick Kiln Lock, no 33, with a boat already descending some eight or nine feet, by estimation. A further turn right, follows the lock, after which there is a straight of a couple of hundred yards, before another lock. In between, the panorama on both sides is over open land, most being used for grazing of horses.

Beyond land on the right, we can now see, as well as hear, the M6 Motorway which runs parallel with the canal for almost a mile, after Boggs Lock. I try to imagine the scene two hundred years before, when there was no motorway with juggernauts virtually nose to tail for much of each 24 hours.

The towpath, which at Gailey was modern shale, has reverted to grass, with the occasional patch of mud. After more changes in direction, we reach Rodbaston Lock. Close to this anglers are in evidence, but no ducks, and only short reeds, in small patches.

Rodbaston lock is different from the other locks in the area. It has a low brick wall on the far side, a car park, and an unnumbered bridge at the lower end. It proves to be no 80, and allows anglers to reach the towpath from the car park.

A variable thickness of trees, gives some respite from an incessant motorway. The canal is now straight for more than three quarters of a mile, at the end can be seen a bridge. Along the straight section, willow trees overhang the path, and our map tells us there is an aqueduct. This takes some finding, and although it is a place where water is conveyed over more water, we feel the title aqueduct, is somewhat over generous.

More craft have passed in both directions, and we seem to have become accustomed to the traffic noise. On reaching the bridge, we discover that it is one which once carried a railway branch, but is no longer in use. Otherton Lane Bridge, however, a few yards further links Farms with fields. This is no 81. After turning left beneath the bridge, which must be a nightmare for the helms-person of any long craft, we see Otherton Lock. This too, has an accompanying bridge, Otherton Bridge, no 82. The lock is full of descending boats, and we make a note that this is a very pleasant spot for picnics, although we are not yet ready for our lunch, so will need to find somewhere later.

We turn sharply away from the motorway, noticing that the field by the path is being used for cutting turf. The trees are thinner here, and we can see the first of the privately owned narrowboats, moored at Otherton Marina. One of these, bears the name 'Serena', which made me look twice, since it was also the name of my family home, in the early 1950s. A special effort was made to talk to the owners who, like most of the boat owners we meet, were proud of their craft.

Several large Oak trees stand along this part of the towpath, and the area is most tranquil. Horses are in the fields to our left, and we now walk toward an older type bridge, which looks like mostly original structure. Only a few bricks have needed replacing. This is Lynehill Bridge no 83, and we climb to the pathway over it, for a coffee break. No sooner had we poured liquid into cup, than a young Fox, seemingly unaware of our presence, trots past us, pausing every now and again to look behind it. Another of nature's wonderful 'pictures', for us to enjoy.

Penkridge is just around the next corner. Close to Lynehill, a housing development was in full swing. It will, no doubt, be fully occupied before this book is published.

Cross Keys Bridge, no 83A is a modern structure, linking the Southern end of the town, with A449 road. Along this section, recent rain had made the path rather muddy, though it was still walkable. There are now other modern housing estates nearby, but the general picture is pretty, with trees to the waters edge, and numerous ducks. The path has now returned to red shale, which absorbs all but the heaviest rain. There are modern Flats by the path, the canal now turns right, and narrows, approaching Filance Bridge no 84. Close to the bridge is the Cross Keys Public House, typical of many such close to the canal, Food and drink are available at normal times, and we think it will be of high standard, as most such pubs.

An oak tree, with leaves already turning to brown, is spread over the path. A carpet of leaves, already fallen softens our footsteps. Very quickly, we reach Filance Lock, narrow and deep, and occupied by yet another descending boat. We are now in what is called 'The Old Village of Penkridge', though it seems, rather like Topsy, to have 'growed'. It's appearance much more that of a town, but we must leave the inhabitants to choose what kind of community, they live in.

The canal now runs straight, toward Princefield Bridge no 85, another full of character, looking through the arch reveals another group of moored boats. They are in a wider section, a British Waterway's development, rather like a mini Marina. Possibly the site of a former wharf.

The towpath has widened considerably, and turns left, past Public Moorings, down to Penkridge Lock. This has a bridge at the top end no 86, which does not surprise us to discover, is Penkridge Bridge. Down a steep ramp, through a short tunnel and turning left to the 'Boat Inn', originally built in 1779, almost as old as the canal itself. It has a homely appearance, caters for all ages, has food, drink and skittles, and makes one's choice of eating place, more difficult.

This could be made the end of the walk, if required, but in order to follow our average length of walk, we can continue out of the Penkridge built up area, a distance of nearly half a mile to the lock at Longford.

Penkridge offers a railway station, and bus services, therefore it is not necessary to walk back to Gailey, but we think this very pretty walk, deserves a second view.

SW

SYCAMORE

Section 4

Penkridge to Acton Bridge
3 ½ Miles

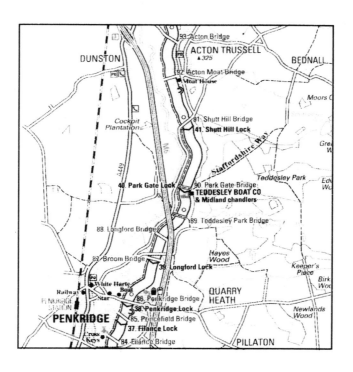

Penkridge is situated on the A449, a little over 2 Miles North of Gailey, and can also be reached by way of M6 or M54 Motorways, or from A5 at Gailey. The final part of either of these routes is along A449 leading into Penkridge. We found the most convenient starting point at the Southern end of the town, turning to Boscomoor along a semicircular road, which crosses the canal at Map Ref 926134 on Ordnance Survey Landranger Map sheet no 127.

Public Transport offers either the railway, local service to the station at Penkridge, or by Bus. Details from West Midland Travel, or one of the main Tourist offices.

For anyone who has already walked section 3, starting here will mean some re-walking through the town, but that should be no hardship, for the walk is both easy and pleasant. Please read the end of the previous walk, from Cross Keys Bridge, no 83A, to the end, at Longford Lock. We now continue from that point.

At Longford Lock, there is also a bridge, Broom Bridge no 87. From there, we see another bridge, of strong concrete, but with no traffic, and no access from either motorway nearby, or any major road. Seemingly, the money ran out, or someone had second thoughts. Whichever is the case, it was an expensive error. Here, the towpath is firm, but has narrowed a little. The M6 is coming closer again, but no real noise problem, at present.

Between the different forms of transport, there are fields which reach to the canal edge, on the far side. As there is little banking, cattle and horses can easily reach the water. We have walked parallel with the motorway for a few yards, and the towpath is once more original surface. It is damp, but walkable, and we are now in a direction towards the M6. Now there is more noise, but as we only have high decibels for short periods, we can cope with the constant buzz.

At Longford Bridge. no 88, we turn left, away from the original course. We notice that this is indeed an old bridge, only a few bricks look as if they have been added since it was originally built.

A few trees stand on either side of the canal, and we now pass under the M6, by means of a long tunnel, shaped in a curve at the far end, to accommodate the twisting waterway. The turn is to the right, and after emerging from the concrete casing, there are more trees, and two properties, one of them looks derelict, which we do not find surprising, when one considers the close proximity of the motorway.

Here, there is a little erosion along the towpath edge, the first for some miles. The canal meanders to the left where there are more trees, which narrow the channel. We are passing through what appears to be parkland, and soon find we are correct, for we have reached Teddesley Park Bridge, no 89. The design of this is rather ornate, and although there has been both wear and repair, some carved columns remain.

The path is covered with leaves, and we scuff our way through them to climb onto the bridge, to view the extensive park. The one side leads to a private property, so we retrace our steps to the towpath, and resume our walk.

We are indebted to Nicholsons and British Waterways for their information concerning part of the history of Teddesley Park, and the Hall which once stood within the grounds. They tell us that, although it has now been demolished, it was once the family home of the Littleton Family, not to be confused with the Lyttleton Family of Hagley Hall. During the 1939-1945 war, it was used as a Prisoner of War camp.

We are already well clear of any motorway noise, and passing through some beautiful countryside. Teddesley Park still covers the far side, but there are farms to our left. After bends, first left then right, we see a boatyard on our right. There are several boats, either in the water, or on land, mostly narrowboats. However, one larger vessel can be seen close to the work sheds That looks more like a yacht, but certainly would not be suitable for the canal. Not surprisingly, this is the Teddesley Boat Co, from where a selection of boats is available for hire. It also has facilities for other boaters. This is the first such depot since Gailey Wharf, and the last before reaching Great Haywood.

Park Gate Lock, and the Park Gate Bridge, no 90, are close to the yard, and a pretty modernised cottage stands on the far side. We found the largest, and most variable group of ducks and geese, ever seen on our walks. Mostly domestic, and certainly interbred, they cross the water, on our arrival, looking for food, although, from their appearance, they are well looked after.

At this point, there is a car park, and the towpath follows the road, very closely, separated only by a steel rope between posts. This is a little intimidating, ands needs single-file walking, also careful negotiation, watching for vehicles coming too close. This section lasts for about 150 yards.

There is a narrow strip of woodland, on the far side. The last of Teddesley Park. We are some way from the motorway, though fields are in between, and further over, the main line railway can be found, though it runs through an escarpment, and we cannot hear the trains, today.

Pheasants can be heard in the woodland, and we are close to another lock. This is Shutt Hill Lock, and to pass under Shutt Hill Bridge, no 91, we descend by the lockside. Whilst we go down, the road which we had walked alongside, passes over the canal. Here, the canal has turned left just before the bridge, straightens for a while, then goes right again. Here a couple of anglers are enjoying the solitude, but no catches so far.

A lane into Acton Trussell, has left the main road, and now runs parallel with the towpath. A dark, well-trimmed hedge is between the fields, and Acton Trussell Church, we think it is ever-green.

To our left flows the River Penk, from which Penkridge earned its name, and it was through this valley, in a similar manner to the Stour Valley, that James Brindley surveyed this waterway.

The Church spire is a high one, complete with a gold painted weather vane. Our book tells us that the tower dates from the 13th century, whilst the spire itself is 16th century. Whatever the age, it is worthy of a photograph, as it is lit by the pale autumn sun.

A line of boats sit in a permanent mooring on the far side, smoke issues from one of the chimneys, and we are impressed by the 'mirror image' reflections. in the still water. Now, we have modern crushed brick path again, a singularly versatile material for all towpaths.

We can see a large complex of buildings over the far side, with numerous cars parked nearby. There appears to be some form of conference, and we conclude that this is The Moat House, now a Hotel, Restaurant and meeting centre. The larger part of the complex is modern, showing a date 1997, but the original, and very atmospheric buildings, are 14th Century.

Our next landmark is Moat House Bridge no 92. It is old, with more recent additions, and there are trees nearby. From those, the most beautiful birdsong wafts over the water, it is a Wren, one of our smaller birds, but their song belies their tiny bodies, and fills the air with melody.

Once under the bridge, a continuous line of modern properties, each with gardens to the edge of the canal, can be seen. The towpath has a hedge running along its border, interspersed, every now and again, with Silver Birch, or other small trees, some of which overhang our way. At this time of year, colours of leaves make a lovely picture.

We are now aware of a group of Swans, making their way from the canal, over a type of 'gangplank', and up the long lawn of one bungalow. There are five in all, two parents, and three cygnets, and they have now reached the window, which is open. Food is being dropped to them, and it becomes obvious that this is a regular routine. A few ducks also gather, and are made equally welcome.

All this time, the canal meanders through this lower part of the village with, what I personally feel is one of the prettiest names we have come across. More properties can be seen beyond the waterside dwellings, and there are one or two beautiful cottages close to the path.

The cottages have vehicular access, along the towpath from Acton Bridge, because only fields are to their rear. Further away, the mighty M6 is once more in view, including a large Motel and other buildings, near Junction 13. There are one or two privately owned boats moored along this slight right hand curve, but being out of season, when we walked here, no narrowboats on the move.

We are only about two miles from Stafford, and are very aware of yet another beautiful county within only a short distance from home. Having descended through five locks, on this walk, we are some 45 feet lower than at our start in Penkridge. We have reached Acton Bridge, no 93 our destination for today, and have to advise a walk back to the start, for any public transport is restricted to local buses.

Our walk has been completed in reasonable weather, with good walking conditions, so our contention that walking is a very healthy pastime, most of the year, is borne out.

Interesting bridges north of Penkridge

Section 5

Acton Bridge to St. Thomas Bridge
3 Miles

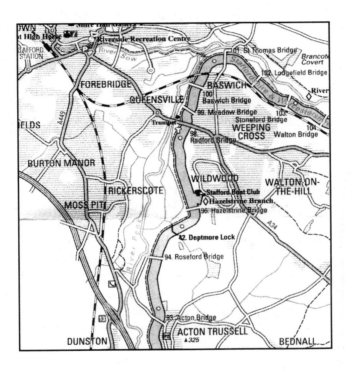

This is our penultimate walk on the Northern half of the Staffs/ Worcs canal, taking us closer to Great Haywood, where two of Brindley's masterpieces join together. Unless you are travelling from Stafford, where you will find a local Bus service to Acton Trussell, this is best done, with your own transport.

Using either A449, or M6 Motorway (leave at junction 13), go North to a very short distance beyond that Motorway Junction, and take a right hand turn for Acton Trussell, locating the canal bridge 300 yards from the turn. There is limited parking in the area. Ordnance Survey Landranger Map, sheet 127, map ref 936195 pinpoints the starting place at Acton Bridge.

Descend to the towpath, and turn left beneath the bridge on a good shale surface. There is a hedge along the path, and modern housing on the far side. All these properties have sloping lawns or gardens down to the water, and the local water birds are made to feel welcome in these. Fields beyond the towpath are mainly fallow, whilst those beyond the houses, are largely pasture.

For some two hundred yards, the canal is straight, and on a bright morning, early in the year, there is a stiff breeze, which ripples the water in places. There is activity on several private boats, and even at this stage of the year, one or two craft are on the move.

Birdlife is active, with Swans, Pigeons and Rooks all making the most of a fine day. We are walking through a flat, open plain, in the middle of Staffordshire, where there is an air of spring already. We can see the motorway, which now changes direction away from the County Town, and also the outskirts of the conurbation.

The surface of the path has changed back to mainly earth and grass, but is walkable, although there are one or two areas of erosion. At the end of a straight section, there is a gentle right turn, then another straight leads to Roseford Bridge, no 94, which is both old and narrow. Close by, a pair of Moorhens fuss in a patch of reeds, now turning green with new growth.

Willow trees stand, as if on guard, by the bridge, whilst near a farm there are some stately poplars. Some barns at the farm are being converted for human occupation.

A long gentle curve of the canal, to the right, leads to a quite considerable widening of the water channel. We appear to have reached Wildwood, although the area is full of smaller communities, each with it's own identity, These are separated from other parts of Stafford, by the canal, which eventually curls like a Bishop's crook round them, in some steep curve.

Another right turn, and we reach Deptmore Lock, with a fall and rise of over 10 feet. Next to it is a Lock Cottage, currently being refurbished, and the lock itself seems to have received some new gates. By the front door of the cottage, a rich yellow colour is identified as winter jasmine.

Once below the lock, the towpath has become rather muddy, which just requires a little more care, but it is noticeable due to so much dry surface for some miles. Willow trees are here, at the edge of the path, and the fields beyond are criss-crossed with dykes, to drain their unusual wetness. For a moment, we might be in East Anglia, with the additional water courses.

We are obviously walking beneath an 'Air Corridor' with almost constant criss-cross of passenger jets adding to the sound of a clear day. They are mostly too high for their passengers to see the winding canal, but we still wonder where they are going to, or have come from.

Unfortunately, the birds we had hoped to see more closely, in the shape of Herons, or Kingfishers, have not materialised today. However, the openness of the countryside is to their liking, thus we must hope that we may still see one or other on our walk. We are on an embankment, a few feet higher than the surrounding land, and every now and again, small culverts lead from the canal into the field ditches already noted.

A left turn, takes us into the next straight section, and we are looking through the arch of Hazelstrine Bridge no 96. The view is interesting with pine trees, boats and buildings visible. Once beyond the bridge, we can see that we have reached Stafford Boat Club, identified by a large clubhouse, complete with clock, and a weather vane in the form of a sailing boat. The Marina contains up to about 30 craft, and is a credit to both owners and management, for a more spick and span club, would be hard to find. Some boat owners are working on their vessels, and the sound of at least one engine can be heard over the water.

Beyond the club, a tree lined bank emphasises the straight and quite narrow stretch of water, and we see the first angler of the day, on the towpath. Surprisingly, he does not appear to be encumbered with large quantities of equipment, and the absence of a keep-net suggests no catches so far.

We notice the tidy state of the nearby hedge, which has one or two gaps, leading to a tiny copse.

The trees on the far side have ended, giving way to allotments below some modern houses. The left side continues to be dominated by wetlands, and we can see a three spanned bridge a short distance away, carrying a road over the River Penk. At first we thought it might be a canal bridge, even though very few have more than one arch, but the canal turns to the right, to a conventional bridge.

That bridge is Radford Bridge no 98, a mere two miles from town centre, and on a regular 'Arriva' bus service. Close to the bridge stands the Radford Bank Inn, a modem well maintained Pub, which has an excellent menu, and a good range of drinks. Many walkers might be tempted to sample the available items, and from personal experience, the service and civility are equal to the goods on offer.

To continue on the walk, one passes under Radford Bridge, and more pleasant dwellings can be seen over the way. Now, there are two paths from which to choose, the towpath, or a tarmaced surface at a higher level. The only advantage in leaving the canal for a few yards, is extra visibility over the open fields, in which, on a later walk, we saw not one, but two Herons. Because of the time of year, we are certain that they were a 'pair', and we were very excited at this experience.

A slight right turn takes us to Meadow Bridge, no 99, at which point, the second path crosses the canal, and we are left with a return to the towpath. Here, we see a couple of narrowboats, and note that the far side is rather congested with overhanging trees. Behind them. houses built high on a bank, must have a wonderful panoramic view. Having walked straight for about one hundred yards, another right turn brings us to Baswich Bridge, no 100.

Close to the bridge, a large, friendly Horse, with a white blaze down the full length of his nose, decides to greet us, by the gate into his field. He is big, but gentle, and we wish we had more to offer, than a few pats, and some friendly words.

Now there are two railway bridges to pass beneath. They are constantly in use, with a mixture of both freight and passenger services, coming out of Stafford. Very soon, we can see the start of the large right turn, to the left of which the Rivers Penk and Sow are coming together. St. Thomas' Bridge no 101 marks both the end of this walk, and the river junction. A busy road crosses canal, and both rivers, in a Northerly direction.

A return walk is not a problem, but if you were given a lift to Acton Bridge, it is possible to use Public Transport, via bus into Stafford station, then train from there to further stations, or by two buses back to Acton Trussell.

View below Tixall Lock

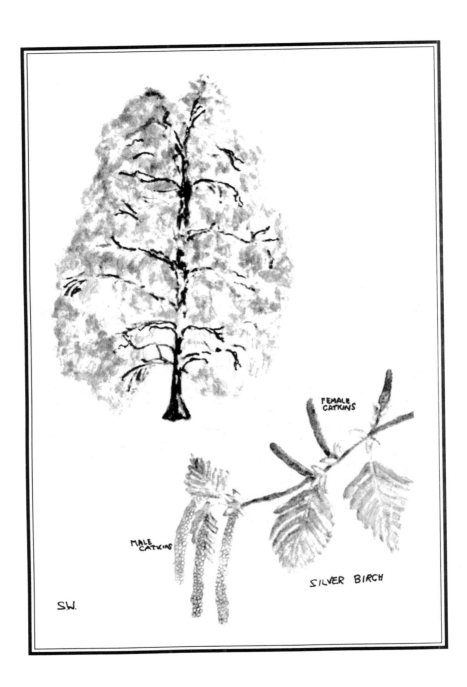

FEMALE CATKINS

MALE CATKINS

SILVER BIRCH

S.W.

Section 6

St. Thomas' Bridge to Great Haywood
4¼ Miles

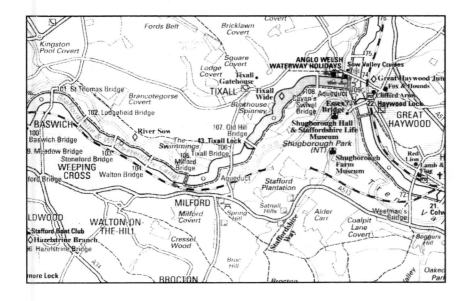

This is a walk which completes the 6 walks along the Northern section of the Staffs/Worcs canal, and is one which I anticipated with great interest. It is possible to get to the start by using Public Transport, but as additional walking is required, it is more practical by private means.

Leave M6 Motorway at Junction 13, then head North on A449, or alternatively use A449 from Wolverhampton. Follow sign for Rugeley, A513 until reaching Radford Bank. Proceed to the summit then take a sharp left turn, leading down, passing Baswich Church on the left. Over the railway line, and shortly you will reach St. Thomas' Bridge. Ordnance Survey Landranger Map, sheet 127, map ref 947228.

Descend to the towpath which is firm and dry, and turn left in an Easterly direction. The canal is running parallel with the River Sow, and a number of farms stand out from the fields on the left. If you look over the canal, a park of chalet homes can be seen with gardens of the highest standard we have seen. There is even one with a zig-zag grass path, which has been kept short during the winter just past. Along the winding waterway, a pair of Swans is noted, one sitting on a nest of old reeds, just below the line of homes.

The railway can be heard, on the far side of the park, and a boat is moored just before the canal narrows, and at the far end of the chalets. There are Ducks along this stretch

There is a screen of trees, along the towpath, and we are nearing Lodgfield Bridge, no 102. This is a footbridge, and we also notice that, on the far side, the railway is close to the waterway, however it is high on an embankment for the moment.

Reedbeds along this section, have been cut down to water level, and the canal itself, quite narrow in places, twists and turns as if in playful mood. Once it straightens, we can see the river once more, over to the left, and where it turns away from us, we can see groups of Swans, a mixture of adults and last year's young, enjoying sunshine and feeding.

Another bridge crosses the canal, with footpath only as burden. Stoneford Bridge no 103 is in very open country and the waterway is raised on a small embankment. Large flocks of unidentified birds are leaving the field, circling round, and returning to rest. At first, I think they are Lapwings, but eventually I think it more likely that they are Wood Pigeons.

We have walked to beyond where the swans were gathered, and find Walton Bridge no 104. We are now in the district of Walton on the Hill, and the church we see over on the far hill is presumably Walton Church.

Soon, a line of boats can be seen. Because of the turn in the canal, we discover it is on the far side, not along the towpath, and this is Milford Wharf. These are moored by the edge of a field, and it is only after we have passed the last boat, that we do see a small wharf. A small winding hole is close.

Milford Bridge, no 105, is a 'packhorse' bridge, which also takes the towpath to the other side. This is the first time since leaving Autherley, that the path has altered.

We are pleased to be walking under the shelter of a wall by the railway, for a strong, quite cold wind, has sprung up, and is less pleasant than when we began. It is not long, however, before the canal winds away to the left, in a series of bends, and we see below our embankment, where the river has flooded large parts of the nearby fields. We cross that river by means of an aqueduct, on a wide left turn, and meet a boat in the centre of the crossing. We follow the waterway into a right turn, and reach Tixall Bridge no 106. The canal is shaped like an 's' and at the far side of the bridge, we find a tastefully designed home, with a large area of ground. Since much of this is grassed, with several golf greens inset, we chat about the possibility of this belonging to a golfer of note. However, our ignorance on the subject of the 'Royal and Ancient' game, means that we remain uninitiated.

Only when we consult the map, do we realise that James Brindley really avoided high ground, since the canal has taken five miles to complete a two mile direct course..

We have hardly had time to determine this fact, when we reach Tixall lock, complete with double lock cottage, and Old Hill Bridge, no 107. Three boats are also moored close by, and we hope the owners of the cottages will not be offended, if we describe them as "unspoilt by progress". Certainly they are tidy, clean and atmospheric, but not over-modernised.

45

Various items of canal-ware, some rarer than those usually seen, are in the cottage windows.

We descend past the lock, the last on this canal, and looking over to the right, beyond the cottages, can see the tunnel, into which trains disappear, on their way to Rugeley.

As we negotiate another 's' bend, we find the canal widening considerably, with banks of reeds edging the far side. We are walking this section on a very blustery March morning with the wind lifting the water into sizeable waves. This adds to the interest, for the various water birds we now see, are up and down, as if on rollers. We are in the famed Tixall Wide, an area rather more like a broad than a canal. Knowledgeable people, would have us believe there are Kingfishers in this vicinity. We shall just have to wait and see.

We have counted more than 40 Canada Geese, some already paired off, and one or two on nests, in the reeds. A Swan flies overhead, its wings making only slow progress against the frequent gusts. Several Mallards leave the safety of the towpath, and reluctantly take to the water.

Willow trees make a thin border, between the path and some fields at a lower level, branches creaking as we pass. There are a variety of small birds playing in the trees, Long-tailed Tits, Robins, Wrens, Blackbirds, and one or two species we cannot identify. There are Coots on the water, and one Great Crested Grebe, and we turn to see a Heron fly over the canal. I am no Bill Oddie, but I know what birds I like to see on our walks.

We have left the wide, and are back beside a canal of normal proportions. Over to our left, we see a large grey coloured building on a small hill, overlooking the valley, and now bathed in pale sunlight. We later discover that is a remaining part of Tixall Hall, built in the late 16th Century. Nearby is the elongated stable block also an interesting building to observe.

A final sharp right turn, where we pass below Cavans Swivel Bridge no 108, into the final straight. We observe nothing of a 'swivel' mechanism about the bridge, but we do meet other walkers who also walked through part of the grounds of nearby Shugborough Hall on today's outing. The final bridge of the Staffs and Worcs canal can be seen at the junction with the Trent & Mersey, but there are still a few yards to go.

Anglo Welsh Boats depot can be seen on the far side, where it would appear everyone is hard at maintenance work, painting, testing engines, and so on. Now we are crossing the famous, and well photographed Brindley aqueduct, over the River Sow. The view from it is less photogenic than the one on our map cover, that having been taken from the banks of the river. Disappointment is tempered with my pleasure at having completed (in stages), the entire walk along this historical canal.

An old Toll House is on the right, we cross the steeply arched bridge no 109, and stand on the path of a new canal.

Walking that one, is for another day, so we sit and eat our lunch, and retrace our steps and try to remember all the wonderful things we have seen.

Long bend at Milford, on the way to Great Haywood

Milepost near junction with Trent / Mersey Canal

THOMAS TELFORD

1757 - 1834

Designer and Engineer of the Shropshire Union Canal

Part Two

The Shropshire Union Canal

Originally called the Birmingham & Liverpool Junction canal

This distinctively rural canal, has one thing in common with the Staffordshire and Worcestershire canal. It was not completed and opened, until after the death of its designer. The majority of the work is undoubtedly the work of the man who was, arguably, the finest of all British Civil Engineers. Certainly, he was one of the most prolific. Living in a later era than James Brindley, his achievements were many and varied. but possibly the most notable, in terms of canal, is the Caledonian Canal, right across the Scottish Highlands. Perhaps not surprising, because Telford was a Scot, who went from Stonemason to Civil Engineer.

The Shropshire Union, as it is now known, was one of his last contracts, opening in 1835, one year after his death. Not only did he design canals, but roads, bridges and aqueducts - even cottages being attributable to his masterly ability.

Characteristics of a Telford canal are the embankments and cuttings, showing that he met obstacles head on, unlike Brindley who went out of his way to avoid them.

The Shroppie (as it is popularly known), an amalgamation of several canals, runs to the Welsh Borders at Nantwich, then follows the route of the Ellesmere and Chester waterway, via Chester to Ellesmere Port. Here it links with the River Mersey, and the Manchester Ship Canal, and completes links with Industrial Centres, all over the country.

Section 1

Autherley Junction to Chillington Wharf
4 Miles

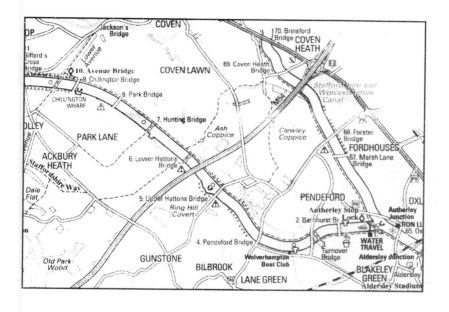

Autherley junction is approximately three miles north west of Wolverhampton, and is best reached from A449 Trunk Rd, between Wolverhampton and Stafford. You are also able to reach the start from either M6 Motorway, then onto M54 off at Junction 2, using A449 South. On reaching Fordhouses, follow Pendeford sign, to Oxley. Ordnance Survey Landranger map, sheet 139, is required, map ref 903020.

On arrival at the junction of the two canals, turn onto the path of the Shropshire Union, under the Staffs/Worcs towpath bridge. You will find a shallow lock, several old buildings, and 'Water Travel' at a small Marina.

The 12" lock is a stoplock, which has no real modern purpose, but it makes boaters realise that they are on a new waterway. The buildings to the left, are quite old and historic, and worth a second look, before proceeding. There is also a shop, with a selection of sweets, snacks, ice-cream, and memorabilia of high quality.

So many other walkers had told us of the beauty of the Shroppie, that we had to investigate for ourselves. Already, the first yards stretched away in a straight line, past Anglers, and beyond the boatyard. Leaving a modern housing estate behind, we curve to the left, and head for a double bridge. First the old turnover footbridge, by which we cross to rejoin the towpath on the far side, then a modem road bridge taking the road between Aldersley and Pendeford.

Already the canal is in open countryside, and after passing beneath the road bridge, we turn right, and see a line of boats moored by the far bank. We have picked a sunny spring morning for our first walk on this new canal, and already some of the boat owners, are on board, completing a thorough cleaning. It is a wide waterway here, with several instances of triple mooring, still leaving a wide channel for moving craft.

The boats are part of Wolverhampton Boat Club where facilities are available for members, and the mooring area is being extended along a road which connects with many different places.

Along the towpath, which is narrow, but walkable, there is modern industry, but without noise, smell, or other nuisance. However, we are soon clear and passing beneath Pendeford Bridge, no 4.

We swing right, where trees have replaced industrial premises, and there are several places where the canal narrows to allow the insertion of emergency gates, to prevent total drainage in the event of any breach. We see Ducks and Canada Geese along the section, and our first moving boat of the day "Nightjar" comes into view. It has come up from Greensforge, one of our favourite spots on the Staffs/Worcs, and the person at the helm, is accompanied by a Staffordshire Bull-Terrier, who seems to be happy, and communicates with other passing dogs.

The fields on either side are level with the water, and we become aware of the busy M54, crossing our path, a short distance ahead. However, just prior to that traffic, we pass beneath Upper Hattons Bridge, no 5, situated at a narrow site, on the edge of a rocky outcrop. There is then a winding hole, and the canal widens once more.

We pass beneath the motorway, noting that, at that moment, more vehicles are travelling from the M6, than towards it. However, no doubt that trend is often reversed.

Robins fill the air with their song, Rooks scour nearby fields for food, and a small herd of cattle graze in the fields. The water narrows a little, and we find British Waterway staff planting some new hedging, and replacing fencing. They are cheery, affable and willing to discuss canal matters. How nice to be made to feel welcome in this way.

Another old bridge, Lower Hattons, no 6, has no plaque to show its identity, and we walk on. Here, earlier rain has made the path a little muddy, so my decision to wear waterproof boots has been justified. However, there is only a small section of wetter walking, and the rest of the towpath is very good indeed.

Now, we are walking along one of Telford's straight sections, more than a quarter of a mile. On the far side is a large farm, if buildings can be relied on to judge. The waterway is wide, and after the farm, a small plantation of trees marks the far bank. On our side, a hedge separates towpath from a lane. Several craft have passed by, their crews friendly and happy.

A fellow walker, complete with dog, now tells us about other walks in the area, and tells that the bridge we can now see ahead, is "Huntsmans Bridge", but I later see that our excellent map shows this as "Hunting Bridge" no 7. I may have misheard.

At this bridge, we have walked three miles from Autherley, but since the next suitable access from the roads is nearly a mile further on, we continue, after a short refreshment break.

We are heading for Chillington Wharf, no longer a real wharf, but right in the centre of private land, with beautiful scenery. The canal is mostly straight until reaching Park Bridge, no 8. and we are now seeing an increase in trees, and the start of high banks, where we will walk through a cutting.

We turn slightly to the left, and can see Chillington Bridge no 9. We walk through the dark cutting, and suddenly, we are heading for a very tall bridge, more elaborate than any we have seen on previous walks. This is Avenue Bridge no 10. We are advised that, the landowners would only permit a canal to be cut through their estate, on condition that they arranged for the bridge to be designed to their specification. The result is a really tall, elegant bridge, which now marks the end of our walk.

This rural walk, is recommended to anyone who enjoys canals, and shows that Staffordshire is as beautiful as Worcestershire and Warwickshire, which are already familiar to us.

Section 2

Chillington Wharf to Stretton Aqueduct
3 Miles

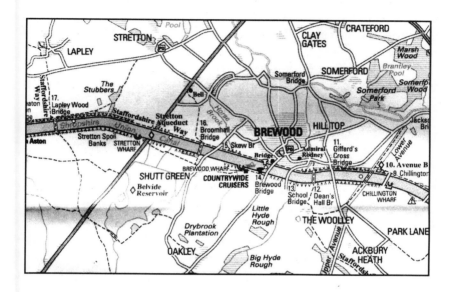

There are buses from Wolverhampton or Codsall, serving the town of Brewood, but no railway link. This is a walk which is best undertaken by private transport, but the Landranger map would enable walkers to complete it from Brewood, if preferred.

From M54 (junction 2), travel northbound on A449 until Coven is signposted. Alternatively, for those travelling from Stafford or Penkridge, travel southwards to Standeford, where the Coven sign will be seen. Pass through Coven, following Brewood signs, but at crossroads just before Brewood, take left turn for Codsall. Half a mile along, at Gifford's Cross, take another left, into Park Lane. This is a narrow road, and requires careful and slow driving. Immediately after a very sharp bend, only a few yards along, turn left into a car park. You have reached Lower Avenue.

At times, this park is busy because locals use it to reach a place where they walk their dogs.

Ordnance Survey Landranger map, sheet 127, is required, map ref 883075.

From the car park, the canal is NOT visible, but walk down the slope 200yds, and you are on Avenue Bridge. Access to the towpath from the far right hand side of the bridge. Descend to the towpath, via steps, and turn right under the bridge. Stop and look at the elegant bridge, it is well worth a few minutes.

Avenue Bridge is the first of three unusually tall structures in the walk to Brewood, largely due to the extreme height of the cutting, through which we now walk.

When we plan our walks, we estimate our distances, double checking with the time we take to complete them. However, it is nice, not to say comforting, to have one's "Guestimates" confirmed, such as the milepost just beyond the bridge which says that we are four miles from Autherley. The other detail, i.e. Norbury Junction 11½ Miles, and Nantwich 35 Miles does not immediately concern us, but we admire the quality of restoration, of the cast-iron marker.

There has been a long period since our previous walk on this canal, and it is now December. It is a dry breezy morning, and just a few boats moving, although others moored at the various permanent sites have Christmas trees on board, with other signs of the season. Many of the surrounding trees have lost their leaves, and although rain has fallen recently, the towpath is generally in good shape, and we are enjoying the fresh air, and the interesting people who stop to chat.

Between bridges 10 and 11, there is a long straight section, and plenty of photographic opportunity. Here and there, on the far bank, are small areas of erosion, but no serious problems, since leaking water cannot flow upwards. No danger of a serious breach.

We now approach Gifford's Cross Bridge, no 11, over which a road enters Brewood. As we reach that bridge, we see more craft moored, all of them privately owned. A group of Mallard are playing under the far trees, and both banks are now lower.

There are craft tied up on both sides of the canal. Most of them are neat, and have people working on board.

When we reach Deans Hall Bridge, no 12, a structure which carries no motorised traffic, and so a little less tall that the others here, it is covered with Ivy, which adds a mellow appearance. Once we emerge from under it, fields drop away on both sides, and over to the right, the town of Brewood stands proudly on a hill, dominant over all other buildings. It is bathed in the weak sunshine of a December day, and offers a photographic opportunity which is too good to miss.

Between the towpath and the town, a stream trickles it's way across a field. A footpath crosses this, by means of a well constructed brick bridge. As such bridges are usually made of wood, we are surprised at the elaborate nature of what appears to be just a crossing for walkers.

Approaching School Bridge, no 13, we see walkers coming from the other direction. Sounds of playing children, from behind a wall, underlines the reason for the bridge name. Many bridges in the area, have the old rope score marks in metal plates, which relate to the days of towing by horse or men, prior to the advent of engines.

We now have another cutting, and, after a straight section, reach the third of the Tall bridges, although on reaching the structure, we find that Brewood Bridge, no 14, is actually two bridges, one for traffic, and a smaller one for pedestrians. The original one is grey/white in colour shining in the sun, and has a railing running along the road.

This pair of bridges, marks the route from the South, into Brewood, and we are swiftly reminded of the words of a local walker from two years previously that "The nicest section of any Midland Canal, is from Brewood to Wheaton Aston." We will shortly be able to comment upon that quite definite opinion. So far, there has been no canalside pub, an unusual feature. There is not one here, but a boat close to the towpath, tells us that in the centre of town, just beyond the Church is 'The Admiral Rodney' where canal users can find 'A full list of foods and drinks' and a helpful map is given for exact location. We have insufficient time to check this matter further, but there seems little doubt that the claim is genuine.

A larger than usual number of private boats, occupy a pretty well designed site, on the far side. It reminds us a little of the Hanbury Wharf permanent residence on the Worcester and Birmingham canal, although Brewood is better sheltered.

Leaving the town, we discover Countrywide Cruisers complete with a series of well decorated boats, many named after Knights of the Round Table. I resist the urge to describe this boatyard as 'Shipshape and Bristol fashion' but it is most beautifully kept.

Credit too to the local council, for rubbish free towpaths, and especially for dog-mess free ones. They have provide plenty of containers, so there is no excuse for inconsiderate walkers.

Over the far side, an overflow runs into a small stream, which then flows back under the canal. Shortly, we discover Skew Bridge, no 15, over which passes a road. We also notice an unusual herd of Cattle. Some of them, including Calves are of unusual colour and pattern. So much so, that some of the beasts appear to have been painted. Our lack of agricultural expertise, can only elicit the possibility of mixed herds, but even the original breeds would be difficult to decide.

Over to our left, is a large, well set out caravan park, mainly homes but with excellent facilities, including a heated indoor swimming pool. It would also be a wonderful setting for a holiday.

Broomhall Bridge, no 16, carries light traffic only, and in common with other recent bridges, it has a good firm pathway to and from the towpath. This is evidence that at last, disabled persons are being encouraged to enjoy the fresh air, and the views.

Although we cannot see it, Belvide Reservoir is beyond trees over the far side. Originally created as a water supplier for the S.U., it is now a private Bird and Nature Sanctuary. We regret not having seen this historic link.

We have almost reached the Stretton Aqueduct, only short and narrow, but built by Telford, high over the A5. It was completed in 1832, three years before the canal opening. Photographs in earlier books show the A5 road to be closer to the underside of the Aqueduct than it is today. We must therefore presume that modern traffic requirements have caused the level of the road to be lowered considerably in recent years. Telford was involved with A5, London to Holyhead, trunk road improvements years after sections of it were built by the Romans.

The original canal title, plus the date of opening, are easily seen from below, or by hanging precariously over the parapet.

We take lunch, with a background of heavy traffic, and walk back to Avenue Bridge, where the car is waiting. An exhilarating day.

Peaceful scene, near High Onn, Shropshire Union

Beautiful Brewood, as seen from the towpath

Moorings between Bridges 10 and 11

Stretton Aqueduct

HAWTHORN

Section 3

Stretton Aqueduct to Ryehill Bridge
3½ Miles

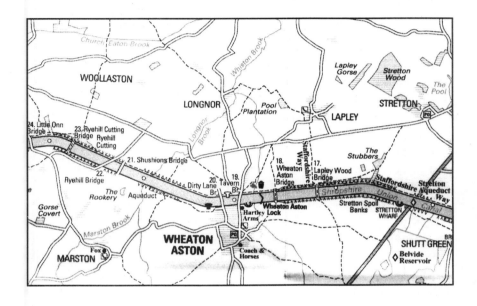

This is a walk which is not possible using public transport. The only bus services pass along the A449, too far away, and too busy a road to walk from that trunk route, along the bustling A5.

In your own transport, proceed to Gailey roundabout, either from Junction 12 of the M6, or from the M54, or along the A449, then take A5 signposted Telford, in a Westerly direction. Stretton Aqueduct is approx. 2½ Miles from Gailey, and is to be found in the valley, between two slopes. In reasonable weather, the Aqueduct can be seen from the top of the first slope, and as you descend toward it, slow down, and look for a small grassed 'pull in', on the left. This is 75 yards before the bridge. Parking space is limited, but there is sufficient room to be clear of the road. You will require Ordnance Survey Landranger map No 127, map ref 873108.

Access to the towpath is via a steep set of concrete steps to the left of the structure, and you can walk along the verge beyond the parking area. As you reach the path, turn right, but before moving off, spend a few minutes examining this small, but well designed and constructed example of Telford's ingenuity. It bears the date 1832, three years before the Canal was completed, also a plaque showing the original title "The Birmingham & Liverpool Canal".

If you are fortunate enough to be close to the Aqueduct, when a boat is crossing, a photograph could be a record of this interesting sight. Looking down several feet to the A5 road, you may marvel at this engineering feat.

After crossing the Aqueduct, you will see on the far side of the water, Stretton Wharf. It now appears to be a private property, in the grounds of a large house, but there is still a small boatyard there. To the right of the towpath, fields stretch as far as the eye can see, although the road leading to Wheaton Aston, is somewhere in their midst.

The morning of our walk was quite sunny and pleasant, but since it followed several days of rain, we anticipated muddy areas among a mainly grass covered path. It is wide and level and presents no problem for walking.

We are in the midst of a long straight section of waterway, and walk for several hundred yards before reaching a left hand bend. Such long distances without twists and turns illustrate Telford's design, and contrasts sharply with the Brindley method seen on the Staffs and Worcs canal. There have been no locks since the shallow one at Autherley, and we shall only see one on this walk, and that is still some distance further.

Already, we have seen several boats, some with dogs on board, though we are unable to determine some of the breeds. Dogs and cats seem quite happy on board narrow boats despite being restricted for space.

The birds are singing in the trees which flank both banks of the waterway, and we have disturbed a Heron which flew off over the fields. How we love seeing this large graceful creature. He soon returned to resume a statue-like position to watch for his next meal. We are also thrilled to see the Martins, those active little birds, catching insects whilst on the wing. They are as much a sign of summer, as are the Swallows, though seen more widely across our canals, than the more acrobatic harbingers of warmth, It was the time too, for Cuckoos, though we did not hear any on that walk. Regrettably, we have heard fewer in recent years.

We are now walking between high banks, through a cutting. Trees, patches of fern, and other undergrowth line both sides, and the path is noticeably wetter. It would greatly benefit from a load of crushed brick.

A trio of Mallard fly up the canal, then settle once more. This is another straight section, in the middle of which, we locate Lapley Wood Bridge, no 17. Along this part of the path, we did find that our waterproof boots were extremely useful.

Already, we can see the next bridge No 18, Wheaton Aston Bridge at which point, the cutting ends, and Wheaton Aston Lock, can be seen, a few yards further. Once more, the towpath is modern and dry, which now proves to us that the worst patches of wet, are sited where water runs down high banks, and that is usually in a cutting.

Here, there are moorings for both private and hired craft, and it is noticeable that the season is already well established, for cruising. Wheaton Aston is a busy place, both on road, and water. If walkers decide to start or finish their walk here, there is limited parking, near to the lock.

Two Public Houses offer food and drink to visitors. The Hartley Arms, is situated close to the canalside, a few steps over the bridge Tavern Bridge no 19, whilst just along the main street is The Coach and Horses. There are plenty of seats along this section, so those wishing to picnic, are also catered for. The cleanliness, and homely atmosphere of the village, encourages canal walkers to pause and enjoy at least a short while there.

Passing beneath Tavern Bridge, we find ourselves in a cutting, once again, but it is only a shallow one. Trees line both sides, and there are various boats moored here. A family of ducks swims down the centre in convoy. Rope marks can be seen in metal posts, beneath the bridge.

Above the bank, on the far side, there are houses, whilst on our side, it becomes more open. We had been told, some months prior to walking in this area, that, the stretch from Brewood to Wheaton Aston, was "one of the most beautiful on Midland Canals". I would not disagree with this, except to qualify the opinion by saying that there are many similarly beautiful parts of our canals.

Dirty Lane Bridge, no 20, is reached by us, but not justified by such a title. The canal narrows to pass beneath, and the towpath narrows also. It is grassy once more, but walkable. We see more privately owned boats at mooring here.

Out in the open country now, fallow fields are on the far side. with plenty of lush vegetation along both sides. We have been overtaken by a boat - nothing unusual in that, but worthy of mention for other reasons. It has more colourful paintings than other boats seen, excellently drawn, and the lady at the tiller told us that she was involved in the building of the boat, some years previously. No wonder she was proudly in charge of the craft.

We have turned to the right, into another straight, and are now on an embankment. There are steep drops into fields on both sides, and at least four hundred yards to the next bridge. We are pleased that the canal is being so extensively used for holiday cruising, as well as by local enthusiasts.

Over to our right, there is a farm with a large herd of mixed cattle. How pleasing to see an increase in traditional farming again. A brick wall, along the edge of the towpath, identifies another aqueduct. Only a small one, and over a dry culvert, and we almost failed to identify it as such.

We reach Shushions Bridge, no 21, through which we can see yet another one, which we correctly guess is Ryehill Bridge.

Ryehill Bridge, no 22, has been built at an angle and is a fine example of excellent brickwork. It is also quite a tall structure, and identifies the commencement of Ryehill cutting, another deep example of Telford's work. It marks the end of our walk, but it is worth the steep climb onto the bridge itself onto a nearby lane, from where a new panorama opens out.

Canal Boat decoration

CRACK WILLOW

MALE CATKINS

FEMALE CATKINS

S.W.

Section 4

Ryehill Bridge to Gnosall Heath
3½ Miles

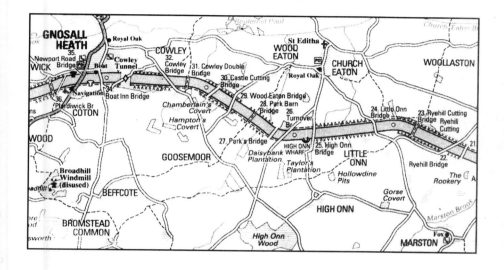

In order to reach the commencement of this walk, you will need to be a good navigator, or, at least, have one with you. The starting point is not far from the village of Wheaton Aston, and if you prefer to start from there, you will add a half mile to the walk, but it will be easier to locate. However, we will give the full directions, anyway.

Wheaton Aston is reached from A5 road (Watling Street), from Telford, or Gailey. (For directions to Gailey, please see the introduction to the previous section.) From the main road, the route into W. A. is best from Ivetsey Bank. Pass through the village, and over the canal, turning left at T. Junction (signpost Church Eaton). In a little over a mile, turn left near Longnor Gorse Farm, and the first bridge reached, is Rychill Bridge. Using Ordnance Survey Landranger Map No 127, your start is at Map Ref 847150.

Do not be deterred by the slight difficulty in locating this walk, for we feel it is one of the best, if not THE best along this pretty, rural canal, so typical of its creator, Thomas Telford.

From Ryehill Bridge No 22, at which point, several suitable parking areas by the lane are available, descend the steepish slope onto the towpath. Immediately, you are in a deep cutting, trees lining both sides (very colourful in autumn). Here, the canal is straight, but turns left at the end of the cutting. A profusion of varieties of fern grow on the steep banks. Pass under Ryehill Cutting Bridge, no 23, and the trees begin to thin out, in preparation for the open fields, just past the slight left hand curve.

Now, you are in a very long straight section, of approximately 600 yards, during which, you will pass beneath three bridges.

Close to the first of these bridges, Little Onn, no 24, several craft are moored, and despite the lateness in the season, we already see others, which are cruising along the waterway. It was quite wet whilst walking through Ryehill Cutting, and we recommend use of waterproof footwear throughout walks on the Shropshire Union. However, for the stretch from the Bridge 24, we are pleased to note that, despite a very wet few weeks, the grass surface is walkable and mainly free from mud.

Further privately owned boats are moored beyond the bridge, and we are now walking along an embankment, above fields on both sides. A farm is beyond the field on the far side, and the overflow from the canal, runs into a small pool, which is sited on the farm land.

We are walking at the end of October, along this section, and because of the continued mild weather, many trees have still to change colour. Those that have, however, have dropped leaves into the water, where they lie in patterns caused by the water movement, and by the wind, which on this day, is quite strong.

Wildlife is limited to a few Mallard, and groups of Rooks, using the wind to take most of the effort out of flying, in one direction, whilst needing maximum strength, the opposite way. These very gregarious birds are highly active, whether to obtain extra food for coming winter, or for other reasons, we know not.

One boater called out that they had seen a Kingfisher, near to a bridge, but unfortunately we missed out on both directions of the walk.

Looking down, we can see on one side, fields which have already been cleared of their sugar beet crop, whilst on the other, they are fallow. More narrow boats are tied at the far bank, stretches of grass indicating private moorings.

As we approach High Onn Bridge, no 25, a large building is being renovated, we think it may be to do with horses.

After a wet and windy start, the morning has brightened and is now highly suited to walking. The autumn colours, though slow in places, are showing well through the cuttings where the trees are thickest.

Our first Ducks in groups, are now seen cruising down the centre of the water, and we notice a white one is established with the group, also evidence (by colour) of inter-breeding.

Whilst passing beneath the bridge, we see the metal posts with rope grooves etched down their length, evidence of the earlier use of horses. The wisdom of their being left in situ, under most bridges, gives the opportunity for new generations to see proof of original transport methods.

The canal is still straight, and there are more private boats along the far bank. Trees are once more starting to dominate the edges of our route, and our map indicates that, shortly we turn very slightly to the right to pass under the next bridge. Along this section, a few muddy patches are encountered. Nothing to make the walk difficult, but proof of the need for waterproof boots.

Turnover Bridge, no 26, marks the point where, for the first time since walking along the Shroppie, from Autherley, the towpath changes to the left hand side. The bridge is not only well preserved, but is a good example of gentler slopes, and separate pathway to the main bridge for the horse changeover. We use the horse route, and descend to the new path, which is a little muddy.

Although we have not seen a Heron yet, on our travels, we now find the British Waterways Boat "Heron" looking rather sorry for itself, rather lopsided. It is apparently used to teach people about our canals. So we wish it luck, and safe recovery.

It is only a short distance along this mini cutting until we reach Bridge no 27, Park's Bridge. This is merely linking various parts of the local farm areas, and has only a track running across. It is what is known as an accommodation bridge.

We notice several herds of cattle in this area, one or two being quite large. So perhaps the farming community in Shropshire is recovering a little from the recession. At various points along this canal, overflows are placed with the intention of avoiding flooding, but even after so much rain, no water is running over the lips, and away into streams.

Between the two previous bridges, the canal had altered course slightly. Now, it runs straight toward the next bridge, Park Barn Bridge no 28. This is also a linking bridge, although it does carry a footpath. A derelict brick building stands in the nearby field, and could be the Barn referred to in the name.

We notice that the towpath, and its edges, have been maintained to a high standard, with all grass having recently been trimmed. Also, the cleanliness is very noticeable, when comparing with some Midland waterways, not one item of rubbish so far, on the walk.

Several narrow boats have passed us in one direction or another, which makes us aware that there are other people in the area. However, it is pleasant to have such peace and quiet, to enable us to observe nature without interruption.

We are approaching Wood Eaton Bridge, no 29, one of the

taller variety, at the end of a cutting, but also, we believe, one designed by the land owners of the time, rather than the canal company. This would be the condition under which the canal was allowed to traverse the land.

It has to be said that, these bridges are elegant, and built with quality materials. Photographs are very good records of the range of colour in the stone.

We are now walking in a very beautiful cutting. Trees overhang the waterway on both sides, and the canal is straight for two or three hundred yards, until we reach another privately built bridge, Castle Cutting Bridge, no 30. The effect of these bridges is to give the appearance of a private stretch of canal, though that is fortunately not the case.

There are still more boats on the move, and we find this cutting well sheltered from weather. Before reaching the next bridge, the canal turns slightly left, then straightens for the final stretch to Cowley Tunnel. A signpost tells us we are 12 miles from the junction at Autherley, and 3½ from Norbury Junction, which is our next destination.

There are boats moored along this section, and anglers sitting in what is now quite warm sun. They deserve it, for apparently at their 8.00 a.m. start it was very wet.

Another set of boats comes toward us, one with what looks like enough wood, on top of the roof, to see him through winter, but perhaps it will soon be burnt away on his stove. As we approach the next bridge, Cowley Double Bridge no 31, we see two more farms, one with a really large herd of cattle.

Bridge no 32, Cowley Bridge, is only a few yards further, and we make use of the provided seats, to stop for lunch. Cowley Tunnel is just ahead, and our walk is nearly over.

Considering the weather at the start, we have been most fortunate, with the beauty and ease of the walk exceeding all expectations. We shall be walking this one again, for sheer pleasure.

The walk from Cowley Bridge to Cowley Tunnel is straight along a tree-lined cutting , until just prior to the tunnel, a break in the foliage allows the sun to shine on the towpath and canal.

Unexpectedly, for us, at least, the Tunnel turns out to be a bridge which is longer than usual. It does have a railing along the towpath edge, but apart from that, and the increase in darkness, it could be any large bridge on any canal.

We have only a few yards to walk before reaching Boat Inn Bridge, no 34, and it is once again within the confines of a cutting. This time, however, one of the sides is made up with modern buildings, tastefully designed, many with conservatories overlooking the water. Along the edge are moored a variety of private craft, which are obviously well cared for.

Trees flank the towpath, until just before the bridge, and a pathway leads up to the roadway, and access to the Boat Inn, and one way into Gnosall Heath.

Our walk is finished, and, as already stated, it is well worthy of a return in the future.

Section 5

Gnosall Heath to Norbury Junction
3 Miles

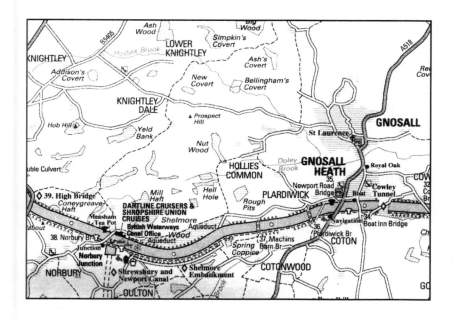

Gnosall Heath is to be found to the West of Stafford, using the A518 signposted Newport. It can also be reached from A5 road once more taking the Newport directions, but turning sharp right along A518, Stafford Street, shortly after reaching the town.

From both approaches, take the turn for Moreton, out of Gnosall Heath reaching the Boat Inn, and canal bridge a matter of yards straight along that road. Ordnance Survey Landranger Map 127 map ref 822202.

After enquiring, you may be allowed to park in the Boat Inn car park, but there are side roads as an alternative, provided you respect residents' access to their driveways. The Navigation Inn is close to the next bridge (on the A518) and is a possible alternative. Please ask before you park.

Either of these two canal pubs, offer food and drink, which is worth remembering on your return.

Descending to the towpath, close to the 'Boat', there are both private and public moorings. We were greeted by a large group of ducks, who were leaving ripples on an otherwise flat surface. It is only a few steps to the Newport Road Bridge no 35 along a section similar to the last few yards of our previous walk, the main difference being the houses on the far side, which are more detached. From here, we could see quite a number of private boats moored the other end of the bridge.

Once through the bridge structure, the canal turns left, in one of its rare meanderings, and we notice it is a popular venue for several anglers. We now see a strongly constructed bridge, which has the distinct signs of a railway, but is now obviously defunct. We now have our thoughts confirmed, for one of the fishermen tells us how, in earlier times, he used to cross the bridge at 100 mph.

The reason for that particular activity was that this angler, now sitting quietly on the bank, was once on the railways. We failed to enquire, in what capacity, but assumed that it was on the front of the train. It also appeared that he was now using his talents, in some official capacity, or other on this canal.

It must have been a main line, which passed over this unnumbered bridge, for it was more like a mini tunnel, at least three times wider than average.

Along the Gnosall stretch of the Shropshire Union, a larger than usual number of benches have been provided for the convenience of visitors. There is also at least one picnic table, so even if you are walking section 4, a few extra yards at the end of your journey, is probably worthwhile, if you have your own food.

The former railway bridge is also equipped with a handrail, along an undulating path, created by many years of dripping moisture from the structure, a process which is much in evidence on our own progress. Once clear of that long bridge,, with the canal still curling left, we see the next bridge, no 36, Plardiwick Bridge. This name, with which we must confess to be unfamiliar, is also the name of this area. We see, over the far side, Plardiwick Manor Cottage, but from our viewpoint, no sign of a large building which might be the Manor itself.

Along this section, on each side, there are numerous trees, some hanging over the towpath, or the canal, and even in early November, when we walked, there was still a regular covering of leaves, although we noticed that autumn colouring was at last taking place. A misty morning was giving way to weak sunshine, and smoke was climbing straight from the chimneys of several of the moored boats. However, no boats moving on the water today, so we were largely alone, once clear of bridge 36.

As we emerge from the cover of trees, at the end of this shallow cutting, we enter an open section along a moderate embankment, with open fields either side. Some two hundred yards further on, there is an accommodation bridge, with a few small patches of reeds at the water's edge. The only wildlife here are Mallard, even though a notice further back was entitled 'The Heron Walk', which gave rise to hope that at least one might be seen, but no luck.

The bridge is in good condition, and leads down from a farm on nearby Norbury Lane. It is no 37, Machins Barn Bridge, from where we see another small coppice. We are now higher in relation to the surrounding area, and where the lane passes under the canal, is a lock gate, not currently in use, but ready for any emergency, for we have reached the first of two aqueducts in this section. Between them is a long sweeping curve, on top of Shelmore Embankment, a very high bank which requires regular care. A breach here could have serious consequences for isolated properties below, and for the roadway.

The second Aqueduct is high over a longish road tunnel, leading like the waterway toward Norbury Junction.

The sweeping curve enters a straight, just close to the second aqueduct, and the various buildings in Norbury can now be seen, even if not yet identified.

Norbury is the point at which the former Shrewsbury and Newport Canal joined with the S.U. and reflects the importance of such a junction by having a British Waterway's Office, which controls, not only the Shropshire Union, but also much of the Staffs and Worcs. There are the usual boating facilities, plus the premises of Anglo Welsh Boats. At this time of year, the main activity being maintenance.

Turnover Horse Bridge

Gnosall Heath

Views of Norbury Junction
Lower scene shows old Shrewsbury and Newport Canal Junction

Section 6

Norbury Junction to Shebdon Bridge
3½ Miles

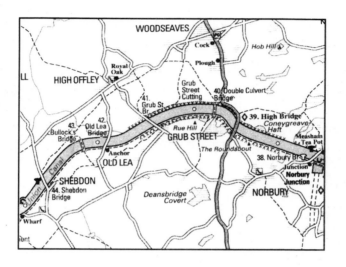

To locate Norbury Junction by road, you should once again use Ordnance Survey Landranger map no 127, at map ref 794228. Travelling from either Telford, Wolverhampton, or other points south of these centres, take either the A5 or A41 trunk roads towards Newport. Those travelling on the A5, will turn onto the A41 a few miles before that delightful town. Do not take a turning into Newport, remain on A41, until you reach A519, to Eccleshall. Pass through Forton and Sutton, and look for a sign to Norbury, on the right. Do not take that first turn, but half a mile further on, at a crossroads, turn right to Norbury. Close to Norbury Village Hall, at a T junction, turn left, and follow the narrow, winding road to Norbury Junction. From Eccleshall or Stafford take A519 (Newport) turning left at crossroads approximately 1½ miles beyond Woodseaves. Then as directed earlier.

There is a large car park close to the Junction Inn, which we note is a popular venue for Sunday Lunch, and of course available for walkers or boaters using the canal.

At the end of the previous walk, we noticed that Norbury is at the end of a long straight, on an embankment, and that all which remains of the old Shrewsbury and Newport Canal is a short arm under the towpath bridge. This now houses boats belonging to the Anglo-Welsh boat depot, which, together with British Waterways depot, dominates the scene.

On a sunny Sunday morning, in early December smoke rises from several boat chimneys, and a variety of ducks gathers nearby for hand-outs. Here, the towpath is modern and dry underfoot, and as yet, all boats are moored and unmoving. We descend from the car park onto the towpath, and turn left under bridge no 38, Norbury Bridge.

Once on the far side of the bridge, we see a long straight canal, with moorings on both sides. Whilst the far side is reserved for private, local craft, along the towpath there are boats from other areas, but no hire craft at this time of year. Fields on both sides are slightly higher than canal level, and we now see a boat heading towards us, between the moored ones which consist of various types, shapes and sizes. Unfortunately, one of these is well under water, and looks rather like a costly restoration job for someone.

At the end of the line of boats, the towpath reverts to grass and is of course now wetter, but, for the moment walkable. From this point on the path, we can look to our left, and see the buildings in Norbury. Most prominent are those of the church, and the Old Rectory, which have trees close by. At the bottom of a field below those properties, recent heavy rains have formed a new mini lake but since the field is merely pasture, it seems to have caused no real problem to agriculture.

Concrete edging, possibly original, is seen along this section, and moles have been industrious along the edges of the path.

We now enter a cutting, where overhanging trees line both banks the weak December sun shining through any gaps, giving reflection to the water, and colour to the remaining leaves. The leaves are so late failing this year, that the last few are still floating down into the canal.

An old cast-iron milepost here, reminds us that we are sixteen miles from Autherley Junction, twenty three miles from Nantwich, and that we have walked a mere half mile from Norbury Junction.

If ever proof were needed, that walking can be an all year round activity, this is the day for it. Probably one of the nicest days for some considerable time, allows us to walk in sunshine, amid the leaves of late autumn, along this scenic waterway.

Cuttings are always the wettest areas of canal, along which to walk, due to any moisture running down the slopes and often being absorbed by the towpath until it can be directed into the water. This one is no exception, and our warning to all walkers to ensure they wear Wellingtons, or other boots of a waterproof nature, is underlined by the frequent sticky patches, we encounter.

In places, the towpath edge has eroded, but presents no real problem. A few Mallard drop from path into water, Rabbits and Squirrels can be seen here, together with several Pheasants which fly high overhead. The sun adds to their colourful show.

The canal curves to the right, and we see a pathway rising from our bank, denoting the approach of a bridge. This is no ordinary bridge. As its name implies, it is a very high one, carrying the busy A519, and is no 39. High bridge is unusual. There are two arches, one above the other, the lower one more or less semi-circular, the upper one almost circular. But, wait a minute, in the upper one, there is what appears to be a short telegraph pole. In fact it is exactly that, and marks the fact that once a line followed along the canal continuously.

At this bridge, another cutting begins, the Grub Street cutting. It also marks the start of one of very few curving sections along this Telford waterway. Although every reference to Grub Street on our excellent Geo Projects map, is spelt that way, I did notice that on arrival at the street itself, it was spelt Grubb, so I am uncertain which is correct.

A rather narrower than usual channel runs from High Bridge toward a left hand bend, immediately before the next bridge, and after passing over the bridge, the A519 traffic, is heard following the canal course for a short distance.

On the bend just before Double Culvert Bridge, no 40, a group of beech trees on the bank, can be identified by their smooth trunks, their fallen leaves, and most definitely of all, by the empty nut cases scattered over the towpath. A large patch of sunlight adds to the colourful scene, before we round the corner to face the bridge.

From beneath the bridge, our second moving boat sighting of the day, emerges, complete with happy helmsman. He obviously appreciates the sunshine, as much as we do. Grub Street cutting continues towards and beyond Grub Street Bridge, no 41, and we specially notice that there are numerous inroads into the already wet path.

This bridge is much lower, and more conventionally designed than the two previous ones, and there is a good access onto the lane above. Just beyond the bridge, it is dryer, and anglers are happily using this section.

A slight right hand turn leads out of the cutting onto a slight embankment, and under Old Lea Bridge no 42. Just off to the left is the Anchor Pub, which appears likely to have been there as long as the canal.

All that remains of this walk, is a stroll between open fields under another accommodation bridge, Bullocks Bridge, no 43, curving left for the final few hundred yards to our destination

Shebdon Bridge. As is so often the case, on rural canals, the area is more dominated by bridges than by buildings.

High Bridge, at start of Grub Cutting

Shebdon Wharf

Section 7

Shebdon Bridge to Little Soudley
3 ½ Miles

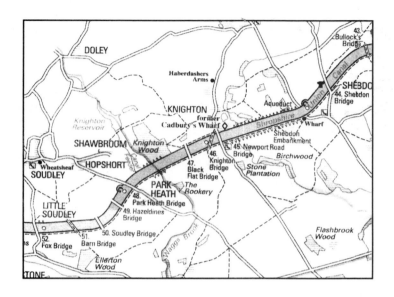

To locate the start of this walk, at Shebdon Bridge, take the appropriate road towards Newport. From Stafford, A518, from Telford, Bridgnorth, take A5 then A41, and from Wolverhampton the A41 direct. From Eccleshall, A519.

On nearing Newport, do NOT take the sign for Newport itself, but follow A41, until the A519 (Eccleshall) is reached. Turn right onto this road. Half a mile from that turn, take a left showing Shebdon, pass through the village until reaching the Wharf Inn. Park on the nearby verges, or in the Wharf Car Park, after permission. Access to the canal towpath by a sloping path opposite the Inn. Ordnance Survey Landranger Map, map ref 757263.

On a misty January Morning, we reached Shebdon Bridge, upon our finding some broken cloud, and patchy sun. There are moorings here, and the towpath is grass, and quite walkable, but later, there will be mud patches, which require waterproof footwear. Anyone who has walked section 6, will now find that they are about half way along one of Telford's long straight sections.

A short distance into the walk, brings us to the aqueduct, close to which, on the far side, is an old wharf. This has a crane and moorings for private craft. Down a sloping path can be found the Wharf inn, but out of season, opening hours are limited, thus we are unable to judge the standard of either food or drink. We have already discovered that hostelries along the Shropshire Union are less frequent than along other canals, so have ensured that our provisions are firmly in our knapsacks.

We now find ourselves walking along a high embankment, Shebdon Embankment, which gets higher as we progress along the towpath.

From our elevated position, we have a wonderful panoramic view of Shropshire, on both sides of the canal. It is a quiet morning, with little to penetrate the silence, and recent frosts are evidenced by small patches of ice, lying undisturbed on the surface of the water. Currently, there are no moving boats, and, in fact, during the entire walk, we see only one, and that, on our return walk.

Trees line much of the embankment, but only one line is almost level with us. We notice quite a number of them, on our side, at least, are Beech trees. From their size, quite young ones.

It was in this early part of our walk, that we met a gentleman, out walking his dog, who we discovered, lives on one of the nearby narrow boats. As is nearly always the way, we found him friendly, interested in our project, and a pleasure to talk to.

We can see a light on the right side of the canal, at what appears to be the end of the long straight. There is also a clear reflection of that light in the water. Shortly afterwards, we can see buildings, and hear the hum of machinery. On reaching the area, we are in for a pleasant surprise, in the shape of canal history. An old warehouse, complete with covered loading bay, beneath which are three interesting narrow boats. Our map tells us that this is a former Cadbury's wharf and although no longer used for the original purpose, has been maintained to a high standard. The machinery hum came from a new factory, some way behind the warehouse, but we are unsure if that belongs to the people from Bournville.

The boats are all registered in Manchester. One is a steam driven boat which states it emanates from the Manchester Ship Canal, the others are freight carrying, with traditional painted tillers. This is a very interesting piece of canal history, and is our highlight of the walk.

Two Herons have been seen this morning. The first by a small pond, on our way to the start, the other, flying over the embankment.

We now pass beneath bridge no 45, Newport Road Bridge, and note the general area to be Knighton. After the bridge, we see our first, and only, angler of the day, sitting along the muddiest section of towpath. He concentrates on his fishing, whilst we carefully pick our way through the muddy bits. We should have been prepared for this change, for we are now within a cutting, a place where any wetness is prevented from drying by the high banks, even in warmer days.

There is now another bridge, within yards. This is no 46, Knighton Bridge, which is not carrying a main road, unlike its predecessor. One or two more mud patches to negotiate, and we are again on a firmer surface, mainly grass covered. Some of the edging along the towpath between the bridges is breaking away. Also, the waterway is quite narrow, until, once clear of no 46, it widens once more.

Another bridge is close, this time bearing the strange title of Black Flat Bridge, and it is no 47. Certainly the bridge is lower than many previous, thus justifying the 'Flat' part, but nothing particularly Black is noted.

Once beyond that bridge, we are again out of the cutting, and though not an embankment, since the fields on either side are level with the canal, we have an open view of fields, woods and farms. Knighton Wood is on our right. A copse of trees to our left is named 'The Rookery', and we pass over Waggs Brook. This stream passes through Knighton Reservoir, from which a feeder for the canal is shown on the map, but which is not obvious from our viewpoint.

There are sheep in the nearby fields, and farm activity, just beyond.

Due to the lack of locks, and similar features, this walk, and indeed the area, might be thought of as uninteresting, especially due to the mainly straight direction of the waterway. We would not agree with that sentiment. Even in winter, the walk has a beauty of its own, and we can visualise that, in spring or summer, with added colour, it will be a very beautiful walk in the countryside.

We are in an area called Park Heath, therefore, it comes as no real surprise to learn that the next bridge is Park Heath Bridge, no 48. We have just turned to the left for the short distance to Hazeldines Bridge, no 49, then right to Soudley Bridge, no 50. The towpath is still grassy and walkable, and the main scenery is typical of rural Shropshire. Although we have hardly seen any ducks, on our walk, we now see rooks, and many small birds such as long-tailed tits, and other members of that family.

We are once more in a straight section, and have only one more bridge to walk beneath. Barn Bridge, no 51. From there, it is only a couple of hundred yards to Fox Bridge, no 52, at Little Soudley our destination for today.

The sun has now come out fully, leaving a blue sky. The small amount of warmth, is welcome, and we feel that the walk would have been less pleasant on a windy day.

Shropshire Union Canal, Winter scene

Former Cadbury Wharf

Goldstone Wharf

Shebdon Wharf - Narrowboat 'Sheila'

Section 8

Little Soudley to Tyrley Locks
3½ Miles

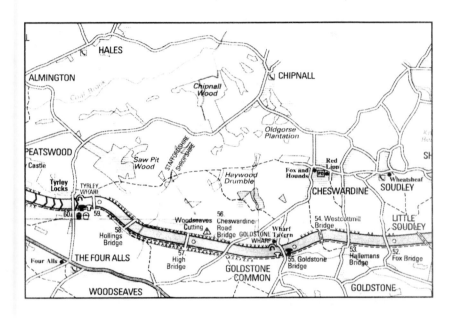

The commencement of this, our final walk on the Shropshire Union Canal, is in very rural Shropshire. All those travelling from directions other than the West/North West, need to locate the A41, this being the main road between Wolverhampton Newport and on to Whitchurch. Just a mile beyond Chetwynd Heath, take a right turn, signposted to Sambrook. In Sambrook, turn left for Ellerton then through that village, and left fork to Little Soudley. You may notice a sign to Goldstone, but a further right turn, 1½ miles beyond Ellerton leaves the Goldstone road, and this takes you directly to Little Soudley. From your Landranger Map, you will see alternate routes, and you may find that Cheswardine is well signed. However, that is a mile or so beyond your starting point.

As with other previous walks, use Ordnance Survey Landranger Map, No 127, and your map ref is 717284. Parking is on verges near to the canal. Public transport is not practical, but 'Arriva' do run local services in the area.

Descend to the towpath, at Fox Bridge, Little Soudley, no 52. You are in open country, and to your right, the waterway is on an embankment. A few ducks may be seen along this section, but in the middle of winter, when we first walked here, the majority of bird-life is Rooks and Wood Pigeons, plus smaller birds in the hedgerows.

This is rural Shropshire, and farms are much in evidence. Cattle and sheep are more frequent, than in other areas, and a few crops, mainly sugar beet are seen. There are, however, many fallow fields, victim of a succession of short-sighted policies.

Just a short walk along this straight section, and Hallemans Bridge, no 53, is reached, but we are now inside a high bank on the far side, thus creating one of many cuttings.

From Hallemans Bridge, we can already see that the waterway is about to turn to the left. No sooner than we emerge from one cutting, we are seeing trees, marking the next one, through the archway of Bridge no 54, Westcottmill Bridge, which is right on the left hand bend, we had anticipated.

In the distance, we can see boats which indicate Goldstone Wharf is not far ahead. However, before that, we have to walk along a grass towpath, which is just about clear of mud, but which

94

is most certainly soft, in places. The trees have thinned on the far side, and along the pathway, there is an unobstructed view over the fields, and there is a small stream running parallel with the canal, for a few yards.

We reach Goldstone Bridge, no 55 and wonder what might be the connection with gold, from the past. It is a humped-back bridge, and we see the Wharf Tavern to the right. No sign that it is open for lunch, in the winter, especially mid-week, but it looks as if it would be a pleasant place to refresh, in season. To the left of the bridge, there are some parking places, so anyone wishing to start from that point, and reduce the walk, could do so. An Arriva bus from Market Drayton, also crossed that bridge.

Good moorings for visitors to The Wharf Tavern, and one or two privately owned craft either end of this section.

As we have already stated, this walk is being done in mid-winter, so that the book can be completed, and published in time for the main walking times in 2001. This morning, we find some ice on the canal surface, and a towpath on which frost has hardened any mud patches. It is a calm day, and ideal for walking The waterway turned slightly right at Goldstone, and now is seen to be straight for several hundred yards. Trees now line the far side, but so far our side is still an open view.

Very soon, there are trees on both sides, and as we approach the next bridge, Cheswardine Road Bridge, no 56, we realise that a large cutting is shortly to be entered. Some edges of the towpath are weak, even broken, trees overhang on the far side, reducing the width of the channel.

When we reach the bridge, large British Waterways notices warn of several dangers. For the boater, an extremely narrow channel makes the required maximum speed 2 miles per hour. There are warnings too, for the walker. Possible bank erosion, landslips, rock falls, and wet paths. Nothing new in all this, except that it is now acknowledged by BW.

It is, one must admit, a new experience, rather like a safari through uncharted regions, except that we do have a map, and no-one else to be seen for much of the cutting. High rocks line both sides, for the first hundred yards or so, with plants growing in crevices and trees above the rocks. After the rocks, the banks are mainly sandy, with the result that there are several places where earth and plants have slid into the water. One or two fallen trees and an interesting variety of ferns, complete the picture.

The waterway is extremely narrow, and for much of this cutting's length, two boats would be unable to pass. We see a tiny Wren, looking for food among a patch of brambles, marvelling at its ability to survive, despite such a tiny body.

In front of us, is a very tall bridge, aptly named High Bridge, and the second, so named on this canal. This time it is no 57, and is more or less mid-way along Woodseaves Cutting. Looking through the arch, there is some mist beyond, but as we reach that point, the sun breaks through, and catches the tops of the trees.

Beyond High Bridge, we continue to pick our way carefully, through patches of mud, and over a couple of sandslides, which cover the path. However, it is good exercise, the air is fresh, and there is much green vegetation to identify, on the sides. The path is only single file width, and in places, large stones are under the surface.

The total length of this straight section must be close to a mile, but we now see the sign of a turn to the right. Just beyond that place, lurks a bridge which is Hollings Bridge, no 58, It is yet another very tall one, possibly not quite as high as High Bridge. Melting frost drips from the trees in a series of ever widening ripples. We meet the only other person seen today, and warn him of the sandslides ahead of him. From the state of his boots, he is already aware of the conditions.

We are past the bridge, and a left turn is just ahead. At last we emerge from the cutting, and see Tyrley Wharf Bridge, no 59 a conventional sized one, just ahead of which we see a mile post, which confirms our own estimates of daily walk distances. The path is now firm and dry, and after the bridge, there are boats moored on both sides, and buildings on the right. This is Tyrley, and we see the top lock and close by, the final bridge, no 60.

The buildings bear dates of 1837, and 1840, which show that they were constructed for canal use, but they certainly do not show their age. Under the bridge, the canal turns right, and the other four Tyrley Locks, descending toward Market Drayton, can be seen.

However, this is the end of our planned final walk, and the completion of our third walking book. We hope you have had pleasure from at least some of our walks.

Goldstone Wharf

Cottages at Tyrley

Hollings Bridge, Woodseaves Cutting

INDEX